Xmas 1992
Copiapó Chile
For Bob

BEAUTIFUL BRITISH COLUMBIA

Songs from the Wild

A Book by
Karl Spreitz

Songs from the Wild

**Concept, Design
& Photo Selection**
Karl Spreitz

Editor
Paul Grescoe

Art Curator
Diane Farris

Production Assistant
Lyn Quan

Editorial Assistants
Brian Emigh
Mary Kruse
Anita Willis

Typesetting
Ewan Edwards (e²)

Front Cover
Mount Robson, Mount Robson Provincial Park.
Art Wolfe photograph.

Published by
Beautiful British Columbia Magazine,
a Division of Jim Pattison International Ltd.
John L. Thomson, President;
Tony Owen, Director of Publishing;
Bryan McGill, Editor.

All rights reserved. No part of this edition may be reproduced in
any way without written permission from the publishers.

To order copies of this book, call 1-800-663-7611 in Canada and
U.S.A. or from Victoria and elsewhere call (604) 384-5456. Fax:
(604) 384-2812.

Beautiful British Columbia,
929 Ellery Street,
Victoria, B.C.,
V9A 7B4

Printed and bound in Hong Kong.
Many thanks to Dwaine & Margarethe Dirks at
Asiaprint/Everbest.

Canadian Cataloguing in Publication Data

Main entry under title:
Songs from the wild

   Includes bibliographical references.
   ISBN 0-920431-11-9

   1. British Columbia--Pictorial works.
2. British Columbia--Quotations, maxims, etc.
I. Beautiful British Columbia Magazine (Firm)
FC3817.4.S65 1992   971.1'04'0222   C92-091555-8
F1087.S65 1992

TABLE OF CONTENTS

Blue Sky — EMILY CARR, 1936

GREATER VICTORIA ART GALLERY

What do these forests make you feel?
Their weight and density, their crowded orderliness.
There is scarcely room for another tree and yet there is a space around each.
They are profoundly solemn
yet uplifting joyous. You can find everything in them that you look for,
showing how absolutely full of truth, how full of reality
the juice and the essence of life are in them.
They teem with life, growth, expansion...

EMILY CARR

FOREWORD

British Columbia: Songs From The Wild is an extraordinary labour of love. For the first time, the most compelling images of British Columbia's foremost outdoor photographers have been married to an informed selection of the finest landscape paintings by the province's most renowned artists and some of the most evocative words ever written about British Columbia by distinguished authors.

The photographers, the painters, the writers — they are the composers of these songs which celebrate the wild world that is always with us, wherever we are, in British Columbia. Often it lies only steps away, in the astonishing urban forests that still stand within our major cities, or in the sudden appearance of a bear in a North Vancouver backyard or a cougar on the lovingly groomed lawns of a Victoria hotel. A fleeting touch with the wild, as one writer calls it. Farther away, yet well within reach for the city-stressed escapee, awaits the wilderness just over the mountains, the expansive provincial and federal parks and seemingly limitless crown land of coastal peaks, forested uplands and great plains. More forbidding, and inaccessible to most of us, looms the terrifying beauty of aloof rocky islets on the very verge of the continent, remote fingers of sea-sculpted fjords, unapproachable pinnacles and far-northern glaciers — where all of us will always remain uneasy intruders.

Fortunately, whether the wilderness is next door or at the back of the world, we have a tradition of outstanding photographers of the outdoors who have long made *Beautiful British Columbia Magazine* one of the most visually striking publications in North America. They are a special breed who encounter Nature head-on, willing to take physical risk, to pack burdensome equipment into the beyond, to travel for days only to wait patiently for a week or more for the perfect image. They crackle through the bracken of the fir-and-cedar forests of Vancouver Island; patrol Wreck Bay on the Island's west coast, where the Pacific swells yield the only waves worth surfing in the whole country; chase a wild blue roan and his mares down a scrub-grass canyon and through jackpine forests in the Interior; stalk the sagebrush, cactus and pastel-painted sand dunes of the vestpocket desert south of the luxuriant Okanagan orchards; and survive the jarring anarchy of rock that is the Fraser Canyon.

The artists of this land are equally adventurous, exploring deep into the blackest forests, sailing unfriendly seas, flying (and crash-landing) onto glaciers. Emily Carr was just such a pioneer, pursuing visions of the native and natural world in her rhythmical landscapes of sky and beach and forest ("Some say the West is unpaintable and our forests monotonous," she once said. "Oh, just let them open their eyes and look! It isn't pretty. It's only just magnificent, tremendous"). We proudly present the first publication in book form of one such image, *Blue Sky*, which was recently bequeathed by a private collector to the Victoria Art Gallery, whose Chief Curator describes the work as one of Emily Carr's very best.

Inevitably, the prose and poetry of British Columbia also confront the unavoidable landscape. Alexander Mackenzie by land, George Vancouver by sea — the earliest European explorers recorded it in language as lush as their new environment. Charles (Red) Lillard, whose own poems transport us into the brutal woods of the logger, states that every major book of poetry about British Columbia — from James Anderson's *Sawney's Letters*, published in Barkerville in 1868, to the present — tries to face the fact of nature or the landscape. So Malcolm Lowry writes about the cultivated wilderness of Stanley Park, Audrey Thomas about the intricacies of intertidal life, Robin Skelton about the glimpsed eye of the deer through ageless trees.

If the artists of word and image are the composers of this book, then the arrangers of their sensitive tone poems, their passionate arias about the province, are a trio of accomplished British Columbians.

Karl Spreitz, Creative Director of *Beautiful British Columbia Magazine*, is also a painter whose work appears in many public galleries and private collections. Austrian-born, he brings to the design of *Songs From The Wild* an abiding love for his adopted province, deepened in his forays as a photographer for the magazine and, for a time, as a location scout for Hollywood movies. It was in this incarnation that he discovered afresh that British Columbia is virtually a landscape encyclopedia for the world, from its snow-garbed peaks to semi-deserts, from its smallest lakes to the immense Pacific.

Diane Farris, whose eponymous Vancouver gallery is among Canada's most esteemed, is the curator of the paintings in this book. She has selected the work of some of British Columbia's — and the country's — most eminent artists, whose landscapes range from the representational to the abstract. "This was a unique opportunity to include the creative vision of painters alongside the more realistic images of photographers," she says. "Artists' eyes often see, and their hands paint, the expressive emotions that can't always be captured photographically." In this context, counterpointed with words and photographs, the ideas of even the more non-representational artists can be conveyed more immediately to the viewer.

Jack Shadbolt is an artist whose work — abstract at first glimpse — becomes more accessible with every viewing. One of the nation's pre-eminent painters, who has exhibited around the world, he is also the graceful and thoughtful author of three books. Fittingly for this occasion, he combines his talents in the following *Introduction*, seeing the landscape with an artist's vision and expressing its truth with a writer's skill. Elsewhere, he has eloquently written about the image of British Columbia that remains the central enigma of his work — the sense of unknown remoteness where no human has ever been. "It is," he says, speaking for all of us who hear songs from the wild, "the edge of my dreaming,"

PAUL GRESCOE
VANCOUVER, 1992

AN EXTRAVAGANCE OF IMAGES

by Jack Shadbolt

Just what is the lure of British Columbia? I have asked myself that question over and over, ever since I grew up in Victoria and especially when travelling in foreign countries — in that quiet moment, say, after the meal and wine in a hillside café under the vines, looking out across the hills to a haunting Mediterranean village, yet unaccountably struck with a nostalgia for home. Or in India, basted in summer sweat, overwhelmed by the tumultuous grandeur of piled-up sculptures at one of the great temples, the thought of home insinuates itself into the crevices of my mind.

Home, for me, means looking out at the mountains from our deck on Capitol Hill, Burnaby, where the rolling ranks of evergreen climb the slopes to the high granite profile of the ridge. Home also means bleached driftwood logs crusting the rim of a white sand beach swinging off on a sharp crescent around some dark wooded headland — and the tang of salt-brined seaweed and a drift of gulls over blue water. And it means childhood in Oak Bay, in Victoria, where we lived in a small cottage, almost at the outer edge of settlement, with fields of tawny grasses extending from the front door to the near woods,

In Fleeting Touch with the Wild

Although Salt Spring Island was not so very far away by sea from two big modern cities, and although a great part of the island had been settled for many years, on our side of the hill we had a splendid feeling of isolation — of being in fleeting touch with the Wild. Even when the place was in order again and respectability once more restored to the fields, fences and home, they still seemed to nestle between forest and sea, as if they were a hundred miles from anywhere.

— MILES SMEETON

RICK BLACKLAWS/IMAGE WEST

MIND'S I

The forests in their majesty
brood above the quiet rocks
soothed by the sea
Lost in their dim recesses
I can know the creak and groaning
of eternity
Winds too high to feel
sway far above
the lacy tendrils
climbing on the sky
while here below
weakened by loss of light
lichened heavy branches
droop and ultimately drop
in moss-enshrouded silence

Standing here
on a lost ocean floor
in the dim tide of grey
almost at my back I hear
time's wicked buzz-saw
harrying near

JACK SHADBOLT
MIND'S I

Cedar trees, Carmanah Valley.

THE SHORE

Lanes of light lead down
to the deserted shore,
the empty standing tower.
Beside the fields of shells
the abstract dance of wind
is spinning scarves of sand
upon the patterning dunes
to phantom runes and spells.

The muted ocean lies
horizoned silver where
no boats will mesh the deep
and peopling swim of tide.
Within the tower the nets
hung salt-stiff on the wall
are sifting into sand,
the bleached door open wide.

So space before time was,
and here we find our end,
see down all lanes of light
this breath's perpetual place,
and in the tower our snares,
and in the fields of shells
our prayers, and in the sands
our dance of love or hate.

The abstract dance of wind
beside the open door,
the silvered ebb of sea,
remain as darkness folds
the visionary lanes
and we swing in the tide,
each knotted current loud,
each sea-deep dark and old.

ROBIN SKELTON
SELECTED POEMS

Lighthouse at Fort Rodd Hill National Park, Victoria.

C.M. MONCRIEFF

19

ADRIAN DORST

DOUGLAS COWELL

Lower Carmanah Valley.

[British Columbians] were necessarily different from all others. They were the only Canadians who had penetrated the final obstruction on the long westward march to the sea. They had gone as far as man could go. Now they stood at trail's end and shared a mystery. For they alone had beheld the western sea and a world around them too big for their imagination, too beautiful for language, and perhaps too rich for their own good.

BRUCE HUTCHISON

BRITISH COLUMBIA: A CENTENNIAL ANTHOLOGY

South Bay, Pacific Rim National Park.

Tide Pool, Pine Islet, B.C.

Toni Onley

Landscapes they were: the horizon (that hypothetical line that separates a flat pictorial surface from Renaissance world-space) had returned, but the elements had been transformed into minimal, ambiguous, often crude shapes; representational (sometimes only by benefit of an identifying title...) but enigmatic at the same time.

TED LINDBERG, *THE VANCOUVER ART GALLERY*

Black and bone-coloured granite bulged abruptly out of the sea... — MICHAEL POOLE

AL HARVEY

West Coast Trail, Vancouver Island.

PHILIP & KAREN SMITH

West shoreline, Galiano Island.

24

RON WATTS/IMAGE FINDERS

*T*his fog was so thick that only the slight sound of water lapping against the pilings indicated that the channel in front of her was still there. The other islands, the small ones nearby, the larger beyond and the distant mountains of Vancouver Island — all had disappeared. Alice had the feeling if she took one more step she might walk right off the end of the earth. Perhaps that wasn't the foghorn after all but the bellowing of those fabulous sea beasts who used to decorate the corners of old maps. What if this white curtain parted now, revealing dragons covered in glittering green scales, thick golden ropes between their teeth, towing the island away to — where? What a strange white swaddled world it was this morning, everything covered in a blanket of thick white wool, soft and wet and smelling strongly of the sea.

AUDREY THOMAS
INTERTIDAL LIFE

ART WOLFE

Bat Stars, Queen Charlotte Islands.

Receding surf at Clayoquot Sound.

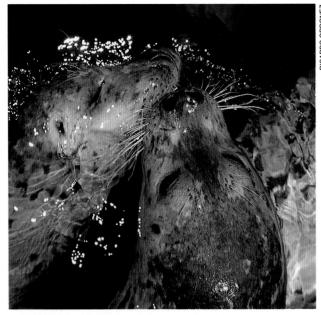

RICARDO ORDONEZ

Seals' kiss.

SONG

If I take you to my island
you'll have to remember
to speak quietly
you'll have to remember
sound carries over water
You must come by night
we'll walk through the dark
orchards to the sea
and gather crystal jellyfish
from the black water
we'll lie on the sand
and feel the galaxy
on our cheeks and foreheads
you'll have to remember
to wear warm clothing
follow where I go
and speak very softly
if I take you

PAT LOWTHER
FROM *WEST COAST REVIEW* 8; 3, 1973

N. DELEENHEER/IMAGE FINDERS

If I take you to my island / you'll have to remember / to speak quietly...

Hemlock, Klitsa Mountain.

ADRIAN DORST

Orca cows, Johnstone Strait.

AL HARVEY

Mansons Landing, Cortes Island.

Sea Anemones.

The mysteries of salt water, deep or shallow, leave me shocked, afraid, overwhelmed, yet urgently curious, filled with desire to know more and understand at least a little. Sometime soon I shall drift again over a kelp bed on a hot still day, looking down between the wide smooth brown ribbons, past the slender dark bodies of massed launce fish, to an uneven hazy bottom covered with sea cucumbers and sea eggs, starfish and devilfish; perhaps I shall see again, as I once saw, a brilliant scarlet squid swimming swiftly, fiercely, purposefully, a headless, deadly body with angry eyes that fear nothing, not even the strange white shadow of the boat's hull above them. Almost certainly I shall still be ignorant, unable to name him properly, doubtful of his life history, groping to name the purpose of his swift movement. But I shall feel again that I have seen something which, for all its namelessness, is strong and vivid with meaning and pleasure quite unconnected with the exactitudes of natural history.

RODERICK HAIG-BROWN

A RIVER NEVER SLEEPS

Sunflower Star.

GRAEME TEAGUE

28

GRAEME TEAGUE

ROTH HALL

Cream Lake, Strathcona Provincial Park.

Alabaster Nudibranch.

GRAEME TEAGUE

GRAEME TEAGUE

Opalescent Nudibranch.

29

Scenic Route

John Ogilvy

Ogilvy explores "the boundary between the city and the bush," which shifts and blurs as asphalt and skyscrapers push back the wilderness.

ELIZABETH GODLEY, *THE VANCOUVER SUN*

GORDON J. FISHER/IMAGE FINDERS

Stanley Park and downtown Vancouver.

VANCOUVER, OUT OF TIME

From the Upper Levels Highway
I look down at dusk,   traffic
streaming into a luminous, vast
aquarium.
         Below, shapes wavering,
finny, striped in tropic color.
Flickers, undulations, phosphorescent
eyes flowing past reefs of steel
and concrete, massed darknesses,
totemic forests thinning to marinas
of masts marking sunken graves,
hulks, old bones turned
in tangled seaweed time to greening
bloodpools of new life . . .

HELENE ROSENTHAL, FROM *SKOOKUM WAWA: WRITINGS*
OF THE CANADIAN NORTHWEST

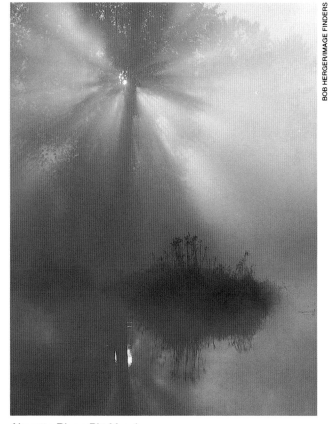

BOB HERGER/IMAGE FINDERS

Alouette River, Pitt Meadows.

31

Chilliwack Mountain

Jericho Park, Vancouver.

On the park embankment they are in the forest, and follow a narrow footpath between the huge trees. A few lone men pass them, walking, each with a cloud of smoke blowing over his shoulder, like little lone steamboats. Vancouver is full of lonely men like this and they all go walking along the beach or through the forest in Stanley Park.

Then they walked on, through a neck of forest and out into a cleared space. A sign read: Bears, Rose Garden, Pavilion, Garden of Remembrance. Children's Zoo. Nearly all the trees in the park were topped, giving them a queer bisected look. A heron, antediluvian, meditated aloft upon one topped tree. Mandarin ducks, as if constructed out of sheets of tin or metal, that fitted into one another, painted with gold, sat about on the grass. Peacocks drowsed in the trees. Squirrels ran about. Pigeons feeding from people's hands. A tame dove. A sense of something unearthly, heavenly, here, like Paradise in a Flemish painting. Pilgrims wandering here and there among the trees.

MALCOLM LOWRY
GHOSTKEEPER

Stanley Park, Vancouver.

32

DUNCAN MCDOUGALL/DIARAMA

Beacon
Hill Park,
Victoria.

Government House gardens, Victoria.

BRUCE RUTHERFORD/IMAGE FINDERS

*I*n the lagoon swam wild swans, and many
wild ducks: mallards and buffleheads and
scaups, golden eyes, and cackling black coots
with carved ivory bills. The little buffleheads
often took flight from the water and some of them
blew about like doves among the smaller trees.
Under these trees lining the bank other ducks
were sitting meekly on the sloping lawn, their
beaks tucked into their plumage rumpled by the
wind. The smaller trees were apples and
hawthorns, some just opening into bloom even
before they had foliage, and weeping willows,
from whose branches small showers from the
night's rain were scattered on the two figures as
they passed.

A red-breasted merganser cruised in the
lagoon, and at this swift and angry sea bird, with
his proud disordered crest, the two were now
gazing with a special sympathy, perhaps because
he looked lonely without his mate. Ah, they were
wrong. The red-breasted merganser was now
joined by his wife and on a sudden duck's
impulse and with immense fuss the two wild
creatures flew off to settle on another part of the
lagoon. And for some reason this simple fact
appeared to make these two good people — for
nearly all people are good who walk in parks —
very happy again.

MALCOLM LOWRY
HEAR US O LORD FROM HEAVEN THY DWELLING PLACE

ROY LUCKOW/IMAGE FINDERS

Trumpeter Swans, Fraser River delta.

Cedar Waxwing, Okanagan Valley.

IMAGE FINDERS

D. LYBARGER

Ducks in flight.

Chesterman's Beach #2

David Walker

The themes in Walker's paintings deal with the celebration of nature (and its ultimate triumph).... We have it in ourselves to promote life and sanity in the world. Walker's paintings are therefore encouraging in their analysis of man in relation to nature. Good can triumph over evil. Maybe we will come to our senses and work to preserve our last wilderness.

ALAN WOOD

PAUL J. DESJARDINS

Town of Yale, on the Fraser River.

These lakes lie like giant dew ponds in depressions at the summits of the hills. The ground rises slightly round them, and, if the hill is high enough, the lake is always rimmed with pine forest, very dark and close. In certain parts of the lake shore there is tulé grass growing out into the water, thick at the shore, thin and sparse as it stretches into the lake. Where the tulé grass — which is a tall reedlike grass — is sparse, its angled reflections fall into the water and form engaging patterns. Where the tulé grass is dense, Canada geese may make their nests and lie there with their young, but, more often, smaller water birds nest there and the geese go farther north.

ETHEL WILSON
SWAMP ANGEL

Cameron Lake, Vancouver Island.

Yew tree, Beacon Hill Park, Victoria.

Fireweed, Kaslo.

GRAHAM OSBORNE

Long Grass #3

Gloria Massé

There is without doubt an enigmatic quality to Massé's painting. Her images do not sit politely on the wall. They are charged with an energy that has the quality of the drama of demons and the directness of primitive visions.

CAROL POSER, *VANGUARD*

FIELD IN THE WIND

The grass is running in the wind
Without a sound,
Crouching and smooth and fast
Along the ground.
The clouds run too,
And little shadows play
And scurry in the grass
That will not stay,
But runs and runs, until
The wind is still.

FLORIS MCLAREN
FROZEN FIRE

Red fox near Golden.

Wild grass near Dawson Creek.

A rainforest creek, Vancouver Island.

GRAHAM OSBORNE

RICK O'NEILL

AL HARVEY

Thetis Island.

A coastal forest needs no sound to advertise the spring's business, no gabble of television, no hourly flashes of news from the sweet security of streets where most Canadians feel at home. But for those of us more uncouth and less attuned to the march of civilization, the silent wilderness is not depressing or even dumb. By its own methods it communicates with the seasoned ear, or at least with human imagination.

BRUCE HUTCHISON
A LIFE IN THE COUNTRY

Rainforest, Queen Charlotte Islands.

JOHN PRATT

WHITE MOUNTAIN

Trees in their glass robes
cold under the moon's cowl.
Arms hold ice.

Wind carries only the howl
of a dog. Ashes of snow
in grey fire.

There is only a faint glow.
Roads of men advance
and retreat.

Tracks fill with snow.

PATRICK LANE
PASSING INTO STORM

Maitland Range,
Vancouver Island.

44

Snow covered snag.

KARL SPREITZ

45

Novembre

Philippe Raphanel

Nature is overwhelmingly physical in Raphanel's vision and her body is sick. She is also angry at her illness. The wind-blasted trees... shake their leaves like weapons in a never-ending war against the elements. These glades are dearborized by means of bilious greens, mucky browns, and a deliberately elusive clarity that makes us think of camouflage.

MARK HARRIS, *VANGUARD*

Beneath the drowse of an ending day, / And the curve of a golden moon. — E. PAULINE JOHNSON

Alouette River, Maple Ridge.

BOB HERGER/IMAGE FINDERS

EHOR BOYANOWSKY

S pring is the movement of stonefly nymphs in the fast water and the hatching of the first stoneflies. It is the stirring of salmon alevins up through the gravel, their emergence into huddled clumps still vaguely orange from the partially absorbed yolk sacs, their spread through the river as fry and the flight of most of them to salt water through a gauntlet of trout and mergansers, bullheads and loons and kingfishers and their own yearling relatives. It is in the slow warming of the lakes, in the steady increase of the rivers as the snow comes off, in rain showers and mayfly hatches, in occasional days of storm and bitter wind more savagely chilling than the worst of winter, other days of flashing life and colour more brilliant than summer's richest. Spring is bloom of dog-tooth violet and trilliums along the flood-swept river banks, it is in the scarlet of the sapsucker's breast, the flight of bandtail pigeons, the return of the yellow warblers to alders and willows overhanging the water. It is geese nesting on the little lakes, mallards paired on the beaver ponds, frogs croaking in the swamps. It is rediscovery of pools and shallows changed or unchanged by a winter of weather, sudden freedom from the heavier gear of winter fishing, freedom from the restraints of snow and ice and short days; it is the whole promise of a new season ahead and the new pleasures that one knows will come, all unexpected, from the familiar sport of going out beside water with a rod.

RODERICK HAIG-BROWN
A FISHERMAN'S SPRING

Lower Seymour River.

Skutz Falls, Cowichan River.

RICK BLACKLAWS/IMAGE WEST

KEN BOWEN

Emerald Lake, Yoho National Park.

Early morning fishing.

Elk Lake, Victoria.

Pitt River, Pitt Meadows.

MIKE YAMASHITA/IMAGE FINDERS

CHRIS CHEADLE

BOB HERGER/IMAGE FINDERS

CHRIS HARRIS

Cottonwood, Similkameen River.

The little lakes of Vancouver Island and the British Columbia coast are uncountable. If they were to be counted, someone would have to lay down a law that distinguished between a lake and a pothole and a pond and a swamp. Then all the ground would have to be resurveyed and all the maps drawn again to make quite sure that no little lake, anywhere, was left out. And that would be an awful job because they nestle in a thousand unexpected places—on the breasts of mountains, in wide river flats, up draws and gullies, on forgotten plateaus and on the round tops of big hills.

RODERICK HAIG-BROWN

A RIVER NEVER SLEEPS

BOB HERGER/IMAGE FINDERS

Bowron Lake Provincial Park.

A *nd how different the forest path was now, in spring, from the other seasons we had known it: summer, autumn and winter. The very quality of the light was different, the pale green, green and gold dappled light that comes when the leaves are very small, for later, in summer with the leaves full out, the green is darker and the path darker and deeply shady. But* now there was this delicate light and greenness everywhere, the beauty of light on the feminine leaves of vine-leaved maples and the young leaves of the alders shining in sunlight like stars of dogwood blossoms, green overhead and underfoot where plants were rushing up and there were the little beginnings of wildflowers that would be, my wife said, spring beauties, starflowers, wild bleeding hearts, saxifrage and bronze bells. Or on some cool still mornings came the mysterious fogs: "Anything can happen in a fog," she said, "and just around the next corner something wonderful will happen!"*

MALCOLM LOWRY
HEAR US O LORD FROM HEAVEN THY DWELLING PLACE

A frosty morning in the country.

ROY LUCKOW/IMAGE FINDERS

Wilderness Just Over the Mountains

If I look still deeper, though, I perceive one more element that I have craved when abroad — the raw wilderness that is just over the mountain rim from my window at home, the sense of the unknown remoteness where no human has ever been. This image haunts me and is the central enigma of my work. It is the edge of my dreaming.

— JACK SHADBOLT

GRAHAM OSBORNE

Manning Provincial Park.

Following pages: Garibaldi Lake and Mount Garibaldi, from Black Tusk. Pat O'Hara photo.

ROY LUCKOW

AL HARVEY

The Lions, near Vancouver.

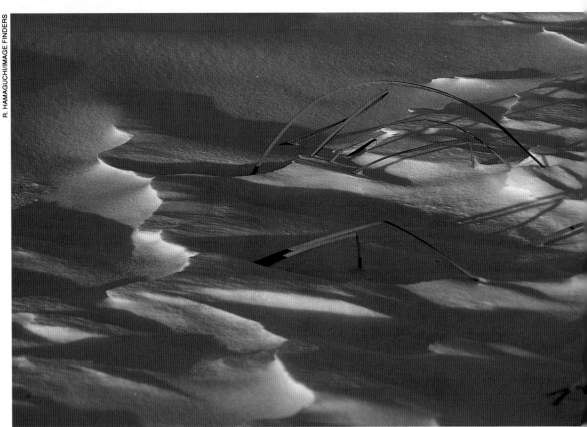

R. HAMAGUCHI/IMAGE FINDERS

Grass and windswept snow.

Winter in Stanley Park, Vancouver.

When the mountains beyond the city are covered with snow to their base, the late afternoon light falling obliquely from the west upon the long slopes discloses new contours. For a few moments of time the austerity vanishes, and the mountains appear innocently folded in furry white. Their daily look has gone. For these few moments the slanting rays curiously discover each separate tree behind each separate tree in the infinite white forests.

Then the light fades, and the familiar mountains resume their daily look again. The light has gone, but those who have seen it will remember.

ETHEL WILSON
MRS. GOLIGHTLY AND OTHER STORIES

PHILIP & KAREN SMITH

Howe Sound and Vancouver Island, from Diamond Head.

Chilcotin Plateau Gang Ranch.

AL HARVEY

Burrard Inlet from Burnaby Mountain Park.

ALBERT CHIN/IMAGE FINDERS

I am on Long Beach, and I am sitting by a campfire, and the long hot day is drawing to a close, and we are loopy with sun and the silliness of the big free day. We have been running on the beach with our eyes closed. You can close your eyes tight here on the broad drawn-out beach and run and run in a lunatic covenant with the flat, perfectly drawn sand.

JEANI READ

BRITISH COLUMBIA: VISIONS OF THE PROMISED LAND

ROTH HALL

Long Beach, Vancouver Island.

63

West Coast of Vancouver Island

E.J. Hughes

Nature is so wonderful... I feel that when I'm doing my painting that it is a form of worship.

E.J. HUGHES, *E.J. HUGHES 1931 – 1982*

GORDON T. FISHER/IMAGE FINDERS

D. HAEGERT

Northern lakes.

Hesquiat, Vancouver Island.

T hen we heard a terrific pounding and roaring. It was the surf-beat on the west coast of Queen Charlotte Islands. Every minute it got louder as we came nearer to the mouth of the Inlet. It was as if you were coming into the jaws of something too big and awful even to have a name. It never quite got us, because we turned into Cha-atl just before we came to the corner, so we did not see the awfulness of the roaring ocean. Seamen say this is one of the worst waters in the world and one of the most wicked coasts.

EMILY CARR
KLEE WYCK

65

KEITH GUNNAR/IMAGE FINDERS

Hunlen Falls
Tweedsmuir Park.

AL HARVEY

Spences Bridge.

DOUG NEALY/IMAGE FINDERS

Flowers covered with early-morning dew.

Yes, thought Maggie, it was lonely but it was nice there. The picket fence and the crosses would be covered by snow in the winter. Then the spring sunshine beating on the hillside would melt the snow, and the snow would run off, and the crosses would stand revealed again. And in the spring the Canada geese would pass in their arrows of flight, honking, honking, high over the silent hillside. Later in the season, when the big white moon was full, coyotes would sing among the hills at night, on and on in the moonlight, stopping, and then all beginning again together. Spring flowers would come — a few — in the coarse grass. Then, in the heat of the summer, bright small snakes and beetles would slip through the grasses, and the crickets would dryly sing. Then the sumac would turn scarlet, and the skeins of wild geese would return in their swift pointed arrows of flight to the south, passing high overhead between the great hills. Their musical cry would drop down into the valley lying in silence. Then would come the snow, and the three wooden crosses would be covered again. It was indeed very nice there.

ETHEL WILSON
SWAMP ANGEL

67

Through a mass of wrack and tangled forest I held on, guided by the dull roar of waters until I reached an open space, where a ledge of rock dipped suddenly into the abyss...

RICK BLACKLAWS/IMAGE WEST

Glacier Creek area, Purcell Mountains.

GRAHAM OSBORNE

During the day I set out to explore the Canyon. Making my way along the edge of what was, in ages past, the shore of a vast lake, I gained the summit of a ridge which hung directly over the Canyon. Through a mass of wrack and tangled forest I held on, guided by the dull roar of waters until I reached an open space, where a ledge of rock dipped suddenly into the abyss: on the outer edge of this rock a few spruce-trees sprung from cleft and fissure, and from beneath, deep down in the dark chasm, a roar of water floated up into the day above. Advancing cautiously to the smooth edge of the chasm, I took hold of a spruce-tree and looked over. Below lay one of those grim glimpses which the earth holds hidden, save from the eagle and the mid-day sun. Caught in a dark prison of stupendous cliffs (cliffs which hollowed out beneath, so that the topmost edge literally hung over the boiling abyss of waters), the river foamed and lashed against rock and precipice, nine hundred feet below me. Like some caged beast that finds escape impossible on one side, it flew as madly and as vainly against the other; and then fell back in foam and roar and raging whirlpool. The rocks at the base held the record of its wrath in great trunks of trees, and blocks of ice lying piled and smashed in shapeless ruin....

GENERAL SIR WILLIAM FRANCIS BUTLER
THE WILD NORTH LAND, BEING THE STORY OF A WINTER JOURNEY, WITH DOGS, ACROSS NORTHERN NORTH AMERICA

Helmcken Falls, Wells Gray Provincial Park.

KOOTENAY STILL-LIFE

Columning up from crisscross rot
(palmed flat by a wind forgotten)
breathes a single bullpine, naked
for fifty cinnabar feet, then shakes
at the valley a glittering fist of needles
rivergreen. And stops, headless.

On the yellow fang of the bullpine's broken
neckbone sits, eyeing her beetle below,
a crow.

EARLE BIRNEY
THE COLLECTED POEMS OF EARLE BIRNEY

Stamp Falls, Vancouver Island.

Takakkaw Falls, Yoho National Park.

70

On the yellow fang of the bullpine's broken / neckbone sits, eyeing her beetle below, / a crow. — EARLE BIRNEY

Yoho National Park.

GRAHAM OSBORNE

*I*ts message is simple, clear as print, and hostile — trespassers are unwelcome. The sunny deciduous woods of central Canada invite man to their open corridors. In the tangled underbrush, matted salal, spiked devil's club, sodden floor and brooding dark of the western coast, man is an enemy to be intimidated and repulsed.

Thus warned, city drivers seldom venture from the main roads before summer. They do not see how wind, frost and deep snowfall have levelled the trees in haphazard patches like the work of a blind reaper with his scythe. Some of the firs and cedars, centuries old and massive of diameter, looked healthy and invincible last autumn. Now they lay prostrate, their huge trunks shattered. In the wilderness, as in human life, the giants often died too soon while the dwarfs and weaklings were spared by nature's caprice.

What savage gales must have roared through the winter jungle, what screech of tearing heartwood, what crash and thud when the giants fell and no man heard them die!

BRUCE HUTCHISON
A LIFE IN THE COUNTRY

74

Rainforest, south Vancouver Island.

Only the ear dulled by the city's rumble is deaf to the forest's distinct utterance — the sibilant breath of spring when wind is shredded through the infant foliage, the summer buzz of flies and crackle of dry twigs, the autumn hush and whisper of falling leaves, and then the tympanic boom of winter gale, music ever mixed and ever changing. Only the nose blunted by the city's fumes will not perceive the astringent whiff of conifer, the honeyed fragrance of blossom, the chaste scent of lichen and hot stone. Only the hand numbed by soft living can fail to distinguish, even in darkness, the separate touch of the cedar's smooth webbing, the rough texture of the fir, the soft female skin of arbutus, the crinkled sheath of alder, the cutting edge of sword fern.

BRUCE HUTCHINSON
THE FAR SIDE OF THE STREET

The Anchor Chain

John Koerner

The idea of the ocean, itself (although we live here, really, on a protected inland sea) is like the idea of infinity. We know what the word means, but it is also humanly impossible to conceptualize. We can only visualize the ocean, and for that matter, the weather fronts that dominate it, in humanly graspable segments.

Koerner's paintings evince a maturity in that they are shamelessly personal and evocative of things that must powerfully move him. There are no other ulterior programs or agendas. He is wise enough, ultimately, to know that there is nothing to prove.

TED LINDBERG, *ARTS & PEOPLE*

...a gin-clear morning sunlight that lasts day long — a day, to landward, filled with new green and ticked with blossoms and birdsong like shards of broken pottery. — MICHAEL MERCER

GREIF-CZOLOWSKI/IMAGE FINDERS

Skeena River.

KEVIN MCLANE

BAIBA MORROW/IMAGE FINDERS

Mount Clutterbuck, Purcell Mountains.

Mountain climbers, Squamish.

GREG MAURER

Nursery Pass, Harrison Lake.

N or was it possible to be in this situation without contemplating the wonders of it. Such was the depth of the precipices below, and the height of the mountains above, with the rude and wild magnificence of the scenery around, that I shall not attempt to describe such an astonishing and awful combination of objects; of which, indeed, no description can convey an adequate idea.

ALEXANDER MACKENZIE

VOYAGES FROM MONTREAL THROUGH THE CONTINENT OF NORTH AMERICA

Reflection of Wolfs Ears Peaks in meadow pool, Valhalla Wilderness Park.

DOUG LEIGHTON

ART WOLFE

ARS POETICA

*To catch what is near —
the deep clarity
of a drake's shuffle
emerging from this blue plate
of early morning water.*

CHARLES LILLARD
DRUNK ON WOOD AND OTHER POEMS

Lake of the Hanging Glacier, Purcell Mountains.

THOMAS KITCHIN

Indian Paintbrush.

GARTH LENZ

Flowers in Yalakom Valley.

STEVE SHORT/IMAGE FINDERS

Moss Pink.

PAUL J. DESJARDINS

Glacier National Park.

THE POOL

The pool sleeps.
The pool is waking slowly,
With a sleepy movement, calm and holy,
Of cool concentric lips widening in a smile...

MAXWELL BATES

FAR AWAY FLAGS

AL HARVEY

Chilko Lake.

Sheep Creek

Ted Godwin

In 1971, when I went to Ireland, I said, "Okay, that's it. No more tartans. I've had it. Finished." I painted landscapes in Ireland, water colour. I said, "God, thirty-eight years old and I don't know how to do a landscape. It's about time I learned." I've always been terrified of trees.

TED GODWIN, *THE CANADIAN FORUM*

... between forest and sea, as if they were a hundred miles from anywhere. — MILES SMEETON

Monashee Mountains, near Valemount.

SCOTT ROWED/IMAGE FINDERS

KARL SPREITZ

Haynes Point Provincial Park.

RICK BLACKLAWS/IMAGE WEST

When the moon hung fat and yellow over the man and horse the dry storm engulfed them with its irrational anger. The lodgepole pines shifted, stirred, bent and flung off thin dead branches from their black trunks. Standing trees, caught and held upright in the arms of those that were living, moaned and shrieked as they sawed like long fiddle bows on the green timber. The swales of grass patched through the forest were tossed in riptides and, on alkali flats, the dust blew.

PAUL ST. PIERRE
SMITH AND OTHER EVENTS: TALES OF THE CHILCOTIN

Chilcotin Plateau.

GARTH LENZ

I want to tell you about the cedar,
the mother tree of the forest.
You make your snowshoes out of its branches,
you make your canoes, you make your baskets,
make your housing out of the cedar,
you can make your plates, the long plates
that the Indians used long time.
Everything was made from that mother tree.

Whenever you're caught in a storm
you get under a cedar tree.
It's always dry underneath
because the limbs is there.
That's why the old people called it
the mother tree of the forest.
They respected that tree.

JOE LOUIE, CHILLIWACK INDIAN
FROM *SOUND HERITAGE* #37

Cedar trees, Carmanah Valley.

GREG MAURER

CHARLES O'REAR/IMAGE FINDERS

KEN STRAITON/IMAGE FINDERS

Deer

*Th
size
dista
hidd
dry b
anot.
Th
chan
the s
sage
tanti
sum
alwa
barn
A
lung
seen
clan
of gi
in th
muc
need*

BRUG

FROM

DIVII

Kamloops Lake.

Dragonfly on water lily.

R. HAMAGUCHI/IMAGE FINDERS

R. HAMAGUCHI/IMAGE FINDERS

Indian Paintbrush, Manning Provincial Park.

THE LAND OF SUMMER

In the dawning bright and clear
a quilt is sewn of orchard
patches, a swatch of vineyard
tapered rows, yielding order
a blue border of beach.

The sloping hills
doubled in the lake;
the sun skates lines
on the mirror,
spins a lasso above the earth

The lake, a blessing
after the barren burn
of desert,
dust-blown, tumbled
oasis.

Speckled by sunspray,
ruffled by the wind,
the soul is put out to dry
in the snapping breeze.

Rattlesnake country,
humoured with marmots,
skeletons stumble
toward watering holes
and salt licks.

Where there is water,
the land is blessed;
where there is not,
the wild grass clutches
at the earth.

S. LANDELL

SUMMERLAND NOTES

(UNPUBLISHED)

PAUL BAILEY

Farwell Canyon sand dunes, Chilcotin Valley.

93

The river wound like a willowing, picture-book road climbing to a castle, and it seemed as though all the world's secrets were hoarded just there, just beyond, just out of sight in those mountainous rocks.

EDWARD HOAGLAND

NOTES FROM THE CENTURY BEFORE

ROGER HOSTIN

Base of Stanley Peak, Kootenay National Park.

Moss-covered trees, Vancouver Island.

MY HEART SOARS

I have known you
when your forests were mine;
when they gave me my meat
and clothing.
I have known you
in your streams
and rivers
where your fish flashed
and danced in the sun,
where the waters said come,
come and eat of my abundance.
I have known you
in the freedom of your winds.
And my spirit,
like the winds,
once roamed your good lands.

CHIEF DAN GEORGE
MY HEART SOARS

Kootenay National Park.

102

*S*oft soft sand, biscuit-colored, and on one side a small lagoon, the water not warm but not that icy grip, that feeling of ice-cold glass, that you got on the other side. On one side of the bay the rocks stretched out in long humps and fingers, marvelous rocks, wrinkled and gray like the skin of old elephants but pocked and licked into fantastic shapes by the force of the winter waves. By the middle of the afternoon, in summer, these rocks became very warm and were lovely to lie upon, facedown and daydreaming. The warm rocks like the warm rough hide of friendly elephants.

AUDREY THOMAS
INTERTIDAL LIFE

PATRICK MORROW

Atlin, northwestern British Columbia.

Myra Falls, Strathcona Provincial Park.

KEN STRAITON/IMAGE FINDERS

105

Winter Landscape

Maxwell Bates

LIFE WORK

I am an artist, who, for forty years
Has stood at the lake edge
Throwing stones in the lake.
Sometimes, very faintly,
I hear a splash.

MAXWELL BATES, *FAR-AWAY FLAGS*

GRAHAM OSBORNE

Ground cover with morning frost, Boundary Bay.

STONES

the very stones cry out
at the collapse of mountains
but only flowers
watch with yellow eyes
the falling of the sun

PATRICK LANE
PASSING INTO STORM

ART WOLFE

Alsek Ranges, Tatshenshini River Valley.

Moose on the marsh, Bowron Lake Provincial Park.

ROY LUCKOW/IMAGE FINDERS

Grey Wolves, Kootenay National Park.

ROBERT HAHN

BRUCE ARNOLD

110   Della Falls, Strathcona Provincial Park.

GARY FIEGEHEN

ALONE

When there is no movement
Autumn seeps into cranberries,
Cool and moist
As a mouth
Hidden by a spray of hair.

At the bottom of this ravine
Someone tunes a drum:
Moose hide stretched taut,
The bell mare
Prancing on rimrock.

In the dying embers
A grizzly stalks
Upstream,
Toward the headwaters,
Until his solitude bursts
Like a puffball
Struck by the echo
Of one quick step.

Solitude
Shifts its weight.
Rising smoke is green,
Green as our dreams
Waking to inhabit sleep.

CHARLES LILLARD
DRUNK ON WOOD AND OTHER POEMS

Hoodoo Mountain, Iskut Valley.

The first almighty fact about British Columbia is mountains.

— RODERICK HAIG-BROWN

ART WOLFE

Mount Robson,
Mount Robson National Park.

112

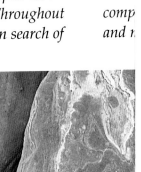

If man does not intrude, nature will repair all the damage. In fact, repairs never cease. Throughout the year, the roots spread and ramify in search of

mois
comp
and n

ART WOLFE

Paintbrush amid rocks, Mount Robson Provincial Park.

Mount Robson,
Mount Robson National Park.

ART WOLFE

Yukness Lake, Yoho National Park.

DAVE WATTERS/IMAGE FINDERS

GRAHAM OSBORNE

Spreading phlox, Manning Park.

Wildflowers.

Glacier National Park.

*S*pring comes early here. When the rest of Canada is under siege of ice and snow in February, it's already warm in south-western B.C. Being warm has a salubrious effect on our culture. It makes us want to celebrate. But you'd never know about it if you'd never experienced it. This is not a feeling or spirit you can learn from a book.

EVELYN ROTH
BRITISH COLUMBIA: VISIONS OF THE PROMISED LAND

Mount Robson with fireweed and Indian Paintbrush, Canadian Rockies.

ART WOLFE

ALAN MCONIE/IMAGE FINDERS

Devil's Paw Mountain, northwestern British Columbia.

GRAHAM OSBORNE

I was ranging out by one of the upper lakes one day, quite deep in the timber. I don't know why, but I remember it exactly. It was like a photograph or a dream that I simply walked into. I stopped and everything seemed suddenly calm, unmoving. I remember thinking it was like a great cathedral with huge pillars running to the sky, and shafts of sunlight pouring down. It was big, fine timber and the tall cedars twisted their long gnarled trunks toward the light. And of course spruce, hemlock, fir... yes, like great pillars in a vast cathedral. It was then, near the base of a huge swell-butt cedar that I saw the grey timber wolf.... And it didn't move toward me. It just stood there and looked at me. I was so close, I could see his eyes; and I swear to you—they were blue, as blue as my own. I don't know how long we stood like that, but finally it slowly turned from me and stalked away.

EUSTACE SMITH, WITH DAVID DAY
EUSTACE SMITH—TWO HISTORIES

122

BRIAN MILNE/IMAGE FINDERS

ESTHER SCHMIDT/IMAGE FINDERS

Turkey vultures, southeast British Columbia.

DENNIS SCHMIDT/IMAGE FINDERS

Moose, northwestern British Columbia.

Mountain goat, Canadian Rockies.

123

Bear Stories

Judith Currelly

Although most modern cultures no longer acknowledge the power of wild creatures, bears still have a way of reminding us that our spirits would miss them if they were to disappear. I dedicate these paintings to the power of the bear.

JUDITH CURRELLY, *ARTIST'S STATEMENT*

...In the dying embers / A grizzly stalks / Upstream, / Toward the headwaters, / Until his solitude bursts / Like a puffball / Struck by the echo / Of one quick step. — CHARLES LILLARD

ESTHER SCHMIDT/IMAGE FINDERS

Grizzlies, northern Rockies.

WALTER LANZ

Mulvey Basin, Valhalla National Park.

GARY FIEGEHEN/IMAGE FINDERS

Waterfall Lakes, Muskwa Ranges, Stone Mountain National Park.

BAIBA MORROW

...They're not snobs, these mountains,
they don't speak Rosicrucian,
they sputter with
billygoat-bearded creeks
bumsliding down
to splat into the sea

PAT LOWTHER

A STONE DIARY

Mountain climbers, Vowell Peak, Purcell Range.

Stewart Peak, Cheam Range.

JOHN PRATT

PHOTOGRAPHERS

Bruce Arnold

Paul Bailey

Rick Blacklaws/Image West

Ken Bowen

Ehor O. Boyanowsky

Chris Cheadle

Albert Chin/Image Finders

Douglas R. Cowell

Greif-Czolowski Photography/Image Finders

N. DeLeenheer/Image Finders

Paul J. Desjardins

Adrian Dorst

Janet Dwyer

Gary Fiegehen/Image Finders

Gordon J. Fisher/Image Finder

Keith Gunnar/Image Finders

D. Haegert

Robert D. Hahn

Roth Hall

R. Hamaguchi/Image Finders

Chris Harris

Al Harvey

Bob Herger/Image Finders

Roger N. J. Hostin/Image Finders

Thomas Kitchin/Image Finders

Walter Lanz

Doug Leighton

Garth Lenz

Roy Luckow/Image Finders

Dan Lybarger

Gunter Marx

Greg Maurer

Duncan McDougall/Diarama

Kevin McLane

Alan McOnie/Image Finders

Brian Milne/Image Finders

C.M. Moncrieff

Pat Morrow/Image Finders

Baiba Morrow

Doug Nealy/Image Finders

Pat O'Hara

Rick O'Neill

Ricardo Ordonez

Charles O'Rear/Image Finders

Graham Osborne

Marin Petkov/Image Finders

John Pratt

Scott Rowed/Image Finders

Bruce Rutherford/Image Finders

Kevin Schafer/Martha Hill

Dennis W. Schmidt/Image Finders

Esther Schmidt/Image Finders

Steve Short/Image Finders

Philip/Karen Smith

Karl Spreitz

Ken Straiton/Image Finders

Graeme Teague

Dave Watters/Image Finders

Ron Watts/Image Finders

Art Wolfe

Mike Yamashita/Image Finders

ARTISTS

Maxwell Bates

Emily Carr

Judith Currelly

Ted Godwin

E.J. Hughes

John Koerner

Gloria Massé

John Ogilvy

Toni Onley

Philippe Raphanel

Jack Shadbolt

Gordon Smith

David Walker

Ken Wallace

BIBLIOGRAPHY

p. 1   Carr, Emily. *Hundreds and Thousands.* Don Mills: Stoddart Publishing.

p. 7   Carr, Emily, 1934. Cited in *Sunlight in the Shadows: The Landscape of Emily Carr.* Breuer, Michael and Dodd, Kerry Mason. Toronto: Oxford University Press, 1984.

p. 15   Smeeton, Miles. *A Change of Jungles.* 1962

p. 17   Shadbolt, Jack. *Mind's I.* Toronto: McCLelland& Stewart,1973.

p. 18   Skelton, Robin. "The Shore." *Selected Poems.* Toronto: McClelland & Stewart, 1968.

p. 20   Hutchison, Bruce. "Corridors of Our Spirit." *British Columbia: A Centennial Anthology.* Toronto: McClelland & Stewart.

p. 22   Lindberg, Ted. *Toni Onley: A Retrospective Exhibition.* Vancouver: Vancouver Art Gallery, 1978.

p. 23   Poole, Michael. *Ragged Islands: A Journey by Canoe Through the Inside Passage.* Vancouver: Douglas & McIntyre, 1991.

p. 25   Thomas, Audrey. *Intertidal Life.* Don Mills: Stoddart Publishing, 1984.

p. 26   Lowther, Pat. "Song." *West Coast Review.* 8:3. *1973.*

p. 28   Haig-Brown, Roderick. *A River Never Sleeps.* Vancouver: Douglas & McIntyre, 1974.

p. 30   Godley, Elizabeth. "Exploring boundary between city, bush" in *The Vancouver Sun.* November 1, 1989.

p. 31   Rosenthal, Helene. "Vancouver, Out of Time." *Skookum Wawa: Writings of the Canadian Northwest.* Toronto: Oxford University Press, 1975.

p. 32   Lowry, Malcolm. "Ghostkeeper." New York: Sterling Lord Literistic, 1973.

p. 34   Lowry, Malcolm. "The Bravest Boat." *Hear Us O Lord From Heaven Thy Dwelling Place.* New York: Harold Matson Company, 1961.

p. 38   Wilson, Ethel. *Swamp Angel.* Toronto: Macmillan of Canada, 1954.

p. 40   Poser, Carol. *Vanguard.* 11: 8 & 9. October/November 1982. Vancouver: Vancouver Art Gallery, 1982.

p. 41   McLaren, Floris. "Field in the Wind." *Frozen Fire.* 1937.

p. 43   Hutchison, Bruce. *A Life in the Country.* Vancouver: Douglas & McIntyre, 1988.

p. 45   Lane, Patrick. "White Mountain." *Passing Into Storm.* Madeira Park: Harbour Publishing, 1973.

p. 46   Harris, Mark. *Vanguard.* 15: 13. Summer 1986. Vancouver: Society for Critical Arts Publications, 1986.

p. 47   Johnson, E. Pauline. "The Lost Lagoon." *Flint and Feather.* London: Hodder and Stoughton Ltd., 1917.

p. 48   Haig-Brown, Roderick. *A Fisherman's Spring.* Vancouver: Douglas & McIntyre, 1951.

p. 51   Haig-Brown, Roderick. *A River Never Sleeps.* Vancouver: Douglas & McIntyre, 1974.

p. 52   Lowry, Malcolm. "The Forest Path to the Spring." *Hear Us O Lord from Heaven Thy Dwelling Place.* Copyright Marjerie Bonner Lowry. New York: Harold Matson Company, 1961. Reprinted by permission.

p. 61   Wilson, Ethel. "Hurry, Hurry." *Mrs. Golightly and Other Stories.* Toronto: Macmillan of Canada, 1961.

p. 63   Read, Jeani. "Pentacle." *British Columbia: Visions of the Promised Land.* Vancouver: Flight Press, 1986.

p. 64   Hughes, E. J. Cited in *E.J. Hughes 1931—1982.* Vancouver: Surrey Art Gallery, 1982.

p. 65   Carr, Emily. *Klee Wyck.* Don Mills: Stoddart Publishing, 1941.

p. 67   Wilson, Ethel. *Swamp Angel.* Toronto: Macmillan of Canada, 1954.

p. 68   Butler, General Sir William Francis. *The Wild North Land, Being the Story of a Winter Journey, With Dogs, Across Northern North America.* London, 1874.